WHAT'S THE DIFFERENCE BETWEEN...?

Vol. 6

A continuation of twisted
phrases leading to bad puns

By Ben Mayo

What's the difference between…? Vol. 6

Can you figure out the answer before turning the page? If you can't, then hopefully reading the answer will make you laugh, roll your eyes, or at least groan out load. Enjoy!!

For information about how to purchase more copies of this book, contact me at: 27benjo@gmail.com

What's the difference between strips of dried cow meat and an obnoxious person with a complaint?

One is beef jerky and the other is a jerk with a beef.

What's the difference between the act of clearing a piece of land with a powerful bladed tractor and a sleeping male bovine?

One is bulldozing
and the other is
a dozing bull.

What's the difference between a rectangular doughnut with icing and a drinking establishment constructed of a certain kind of wood?

One is a maple bar and the other is a bar made of maple.

What's the difference between a small store selling fashionable clothes or accessories and a piece of tropical hardwood used to shoot arrows?

One is a boutique
and the other
is a teak bow.

What's the difference between a low-calorie version of creamy chocolate candy and to fib about your eating habits when you are supposedly trying to lose weight?

One is diet fudge and the other is to fudge on a diet.

What's the difference between a work schedule from mid-afternoon to around midnight and moving from side to side in a hanging seat often found at a playground?

One is a swing shift
and the other is
to shift a swing.

What's the difference between the area of a firearm that feeds ammunition into the chamber and a periodical about very strong or muscular arms?

One is a gun magazine and the other is a magazine about guns.

What's the difference between a person who is the head of a group of faculty all of the same discipline and a section of a store that has items pertaining to sitting down?

One is a department chair and the other is a chair department.

What's the difference between an upholstered seat for two or more people, usually with a back as well as arms, and dishes, typically made of china or silver, used for serving a hot drink made from infused leaves?

One is a settee

and the other

is a tea set.

What's the
difference
between
America's favorite
pastime and a
fancy dance
at an army
headquarters?

One is baseball
and the other is
a ball at a base.

What's the difference between the final phrase or sentence of a joke and a column of folks waiting to be served a fruity drink?

One is a punchline
and the other is a
line at the punch.

What's the difference between the location where someone lives and a commercial for a gown?

One is an address
and the other
is a dress ad.

What's the difference between a frozen dessert made by combining fruit juice with milk or cream and a wager that's certain?

One is sherbet
and the other is
a bet that's sure.

What's the difference between doing extremely poorly on an exam and determining the effectiveness of a nuclear weapon?

One is to bomb a
test and the other
is to test a bomb.

What's the difference between a knight's young attendant whose name is written in an official record due to committing a crime and a story on one side of a sheet of paper bound in covers?

One is a booked page and the other is a one-page book.

What's the difference between nonsense and a bathed pig?

One is hogwash
and the other is
a washed hog.

What's the difference between listing something on the internet in hopes of selling it and putting one more vertical timber in a fence?

One is posting an ad and the other is adding a post.

What's the difference between dispensing or applying medicine and a clergy commercial?

One is to administer
and the other is
a minister ad.

What's the difference between wanting to know about a music recording and a banknote that pays dividends?

One is interest in a CD and the other is a CD with interest.

What's the difference between a large clam found along the west coast of North America and a drake that is all sticky?

One is a geoduck (pronounced "gooey duck") and the other is a duck that is gooey.

What's the difference between making a wide search to find food or provisions and being older than three but not yet five?

One is to forage

and the other

is age four.

What's the difference between devices worn to make sounds more audible and a government assistant having an informal court proceeding?

One is hearing aids and the other is an aide's hearing.

What's the difference between drilling a small circle in a piece of wood and an entire wild pig?

One is to bore a hole and the other is a whole boar.

What's the difference between hair growing in a V-shape in the middle of your forehead and to glance quickly at women whose husbands are deceased?

One is a widow's peak and the other is to peek at widows.

What's the difference between a cat and an amount of money you pay a bank to keep credit available for your use?

One is a feline

and the other

is a line fee.

What's the difference between a dessert made with dark fruit filling covered with dumplings and a shoemaker you lay to rest beneath the ground?

One is berry cobbler and the other is a cobbler you bury?

What's the difference between the name of a big African cat that is tan with black spots and a swindler?

One is cheetah and
the other is a cheat.

What's the difference between window coverings with horizontal slats and sightless people from a city in Italy who use boats to get around?

One is venetian blinds and the other is blind Venetians.

What's the difference between being wary because of a previous bad experience and a bashful firearm?

One is gun-shy
and the other
is a shy gun.

What's the difference between an android and someone purchasing a line of seats at an event?

One is a robot
and the other
bought a row.

What's the difference between an extremely crowded dwelling and a poker hand made up of three kings followed by two tens?

One is a houseful
and the other
is a full house.

What's the difference between long thin pieces of wood in the back of a truck and a game where the object is to remove a long plastic rod from a pile without disturbing the others?

One is sticks in a pickup and the other is Pick-up Sticks.

What's the difference between small pieces of wood clicked together during a Spanish dance and applying meshed material to a plaster shell surrounding a broken leg?

One is a castanet
and the other is
to net a cast.

What's the difference between an infatuation during adolescence and having affection for a young dog?

One is puppy love and the other is to love a puppy.

What's the difference between a pig roasting on a skewer and someone expectorating on a dull, tiresome person?

One is a boar on a spit and the other spits on a bore.

What's the difference between outdoor meals on blankets and a New York basketball team's draft choice?

One is picnics
and the other
is a Knicks pick.

What's the
difference between
relentless fat under
the skin that causes
dimpling and
a lamp one
exchanges
for cash?

One is cellulite
and the other is
a light you sell.

What's the
difference between
tall plants with
purplish flowers and
someone pawning a
Christmas plant that
has red berries?

One is hollyhocks
and the other
hocks holly.

What's the difference between a postponement and a woman?

One is a delay
and the other
is a lady.

What's the difference between the ending of a show that leaves an audience on the edge of their seats and a triangular piece of wire used to hold clothing on a vertical rock face?

One is a cliffhanger and the other is a hanger on a cliff.

What's the difference between hair that grows in a different direction from the rest and a defeated female bovine?

One is a cowlick
and the other is
a licked cow.

What's the difference between a fungus that grows between toes and a lower appendage of a sports participant?

One is athlete's foot and the other is a foot of an athlete.

What's the difference between an unusually large harvest and cutting short the bar used to protect the front of a car in a crash?

One is a bumper crop and the other is to crop a bumper.

What's the difference between an awe-inspiring or majestic feeling and a citrusy green colored underwater vessel?

One is sublime
and the other
is a lime sub.

What's the difference between Pooh Bear's favorite food and the joint connecting the thigh bone to the shin bone of Attila?

One is honey and
the other is the
knee of a Hun.

What's the
difference
between the area
under your belt
and a straight path
of garbage?

One is a waistline
and the other is
a line of waste.

What's the difference between a wasp and a coat that's butter colored?

One is a yellow
jacket and the
other is a jacket
that's yellow.

What's the difference between an English policeman who is in charge and a penny-colored venomous snake?

One is a head
copper and the
other is a
copperhead.

What's the difference between an answer to a math problem that is not an even number and a strange mixture of chemicals?

One is a solution that is odd and the other is an odd solution.

What's the difference between a strong alcoholic drink and a rigid strip of leather used to hold up your pants?

One is a stiff belt
and the other is
a belt that is stiff.

What's the difference between a weed commonly causing punctures in bicycle tires and the main ram of the herd?

One is a goat head
and the other is
the head goat.

What's the difference between the nautical description of a location twelve feet under water and something that is very difficult to understand?

One is two fathoms
deep and the other
is too deep
to fathom.

What's the difference between dying and the pail you strike with your foot?

One is you kick the bucket and the other is the bucket you kick.

What's the difference between looking up to someone and a commercial for a piece of swampy ground?

One is to admire
and the other
is a mire ad.

What's the difference between one, two, three, etc. and a group of professional baseball players from St. Louis?

One is cardinal numbers and the other is a number of Cardinals.

What's the difference between the time following a cafeteria disaster during a morning meal and an algebra class following a quick pause?

One is a breakfast aftermath and the other is math after a fast break.

What's the difference between fifty plus fifty and to fear Attila?

One is a hundred
and the other is
to dread a Hun.

What's the difference between a poisonous fungus and a three-legged seat pulled with a rope?

One is a toadstool
and the other is
a stool towed.

What's the difference between putting a piece of correspondence in a post office drop box and an "M" rather than an "F" checked on a form?

One is to mail a letter and the other is the letter for "male."

What's the difference between the capital of Idaho and why young girls look at young men?

One is Boise
and the other
is to see boys.

What's the difference between the current capital of Illinois and a piece of land covered with bouncy metal objects?

One is Springfield and the other is a field of springs.

What's the difference between a valley in California known for wine production and a dad snooze?

One is Napa

and the other

is a pa nap.

What's the difference between a major city in Florida located on a bay and Dad using a shovel to push the dirt down around a fence post?

One is Tampa
and the other
is Pa tamps.

What's the difference between the capital of Iraq and Father's paper sack?

One is Baghdad
and the other
is Dad's bag.

What's the difference between a make-believe situation and observing a wind blowing machine?

One is a fantasy and the other is to see a fan.

What's the difference between one of Santa's sleigh pullers and precious precipitation?

One is a reindeer
and the other
is dear rain.

What's the difference between a mythological bird that rose from the ashes and a charge incurred from a New York basketball team?

One is a phoenix
and the other
is a Knicks fee.

What's the difference between building something by improvising with material on hand and a dishonestly manipulated group asked to reach a verdict?

One is jury rigged and the other is a rigged jury.

What's the
difference between
a piece of data that
differs greatly from
other data and a
teller of falsehoods
being removed
from the premises?

One is an outlier
and the other is
a liar that's out.

What's the difference between a manager and a shade on a cap that is fantastic?

One is a supervisor and the other is a visor that's super.

What's the difference between a teenager who hangs out at shopping outlets to socialize and a large mouse-like rodent that has been torn to pieces?

One is a mall rat
and the other is
a rat mauled.

What's the difference between grape preserves and a felon improvising while playing rhythm guitar?

One is concord jam and the other is a con who jams on chords.

What's the difference between a young hen raised for meat production and a cowardly Franciscan (similar to a monk)?

One is a fryer
chicken and
the other is a
chicken friar.

What's the difference between the celestial body named for the god of war and someone spoiling the scheme of something?

One is the planet Mars and the other mars its plan.

What's the difference between a marsh down south where the crawfish live and what one does upon finding a bargain to purchase?

One is a bayou

and the other

is "You buy."

What's the difference between what NASA uses to launch satellites and describing something that is awesome?

One is rockets
and the other
is "It rocks."

What's the difference between one who travels from place to place without a home and an angry denial?

One is a nomad
and the other
is a mad "no."

What's the difference between the king's oldest son and something tossed upwards?

One is heir to the throne and the other is thrown in the air.

What's the difference between recommendations and a commercial for sinful behavior?

One is advice
and the other
is a vice ad.

What's the difference between a deep body of water in a dormant southern Oregon volcano and a Los Angeles basketball team's wooden box?

One is Crater Lake and the other is a Laker's crate.

What's the difference between a piece of paper telling you that you're fired and a woman's undergarment that is pale red?

One is a pink slip
and the other is
a slip that's pink.

What's the difference between preserves made from small round red berries and a pile of logs preventing the flow of a river?

One is currant jam
and the other jams
the current.

What's the difference between a brand of the pain reliever acetaminophen and a room covered with ceramic squares?

One is Tylenol

and the other

is all in tile.

What's the difference between a key kingdom in ancient Mesopotamia and green turf gibberish?

One is Babylon
and the other
is lawn babble.

What's the difference between someone finding entertainment in gelatinous canned meat and the junk e-mail of a person who inspires a creative artist?

One is amused by spam and the other is spam of a muse.

What's the difference between being reluctant to give one's location while in eastern Asia and to align the colored carp in a pond?

One is to be coy
in the Orient and
the other is to
orient the koi.

What's the difference between a street that has a fee for traveling on it and someone who galloped on a horse to the sound of a bell?

One is a toll road and the other rode to a toll.

What's the difference between purchasing merchandise and what people say when parting?

One is to buy goods and the other is goodbyes.

What's the difference between an old-fashioned way of saying goodbye and public assistance for those in need?

One is "farewell"
and the other
is welfare.

What's the difference between a document with instructions for medical treatment when a person is unable to give consent and someone who wouldn't mind continuing to breathe?

One is a living will and the other is willing to live.

What's the difference between Alvin's brothers and a friar's potato slice cooked in vegetable oil?

One is chipmunks
and the other is
a monk's chip.

What's the difference between using a pole with a string to catch ugly beings who live under a bridge and putting a line in the water behind a moving boat in order to catch a trout?

183

One is fishing for trolls and the other is trolling for fish.

What's the difference between a group of penny-pinching scrooges and a bunched-up pile of nylon pants worn by gymnasts?

One is tightwads

and the other is

a wad of tights.

What's the difference between someone who is categorized too rigidly and hanging onto a bird used to carry messages?

One is pigeonholed
and the other is
to hold a pigeon.

What's the difference between a boxer who is knocked unconscious and a description of freezing weather?

One is out cold
and the other
is "cold out."

What's the difference between a boat with two parallel hulls and what you'd say if your mother drove a certain company's bulldozer?

One is a catamaran and the other is "Ma ran a Cat."

What's the difference between a Chinese calculating tool and to use profanity towards a Swedish pop group?

One is an abacus and the other is to cuss at ABBA.

What's the difference between someone who failed to remember and someone who received two pairs?

One forgot and

the other got four.

What's the difference between a temporary stop and Dad's underwear?

One is a brief pause
and the other
is Pa's briefs.

What's the difference between stopping work and the remainder of the money gotten from a heist?

One is to take a rest and the other is the rest of the take.